Yes, I'm Adopted!

Written by Sharlie Zinniger

Illustrated by Tiffany Cunliffe

For my two sweet boys T & Z and their amazing
birthmothers who helped make me a mom.

~S.Z.

For my three little miracles A, L, & J and

their incredibly selfless birthmothers.

~T.C.

Some people say I'm different,
But you can clearly see

That really I am special,
It's just the way to be.

You see, I have a birthmother
Who placed me with loving care.

This means I am adopted
Like my fave hero man.

Who found family here on earth,
Now I'm his super fan.

And join their family right away;
They didn't know where from.

Many kids
are adopted
From lands both
near and far.

Some parents take
trains and planes:
Some meet their
kids by car.

My family is not
so different;
We eat, and
sleep, and play.

We spend lots of time together
And laugh each and every day.

Yes, adoption makes me special.

It means that I am loved.

For after all, my adoption
Was planned by God above.

Sharlie is pleased to be merging her love of books with her enthusiasm for adoption in, *Yes, I'm Adopted*. She and her husband have been blessed to be able to adopt their two sons. Together they like to travel, spend time at the park, read books, and make pizza. Find out more at www.sharliezinniger.com.

Tiffany is a former art teacher turned stay at home mom. She and her husband have adopted three children. They share a passion for adoption, and they consider it one of their greatest blessings. As a family they enjoy dance parties, doing creative projects, spending time with family and friends, exploring, and taking Sunday walks.

Made in the USA
Lexington, KY
09 December 2014